Analysis of The Flaw
In
Laissez Faire Capitalism

by

Duard L Pruitt

Table of Contents

***

The Flaw in Laissez Faire Capitalism

Our ongoing, never ending, national financial problem is that Laissez Faire Capitalism is unstable and is also a sort of cheating mechanism which robs from the poor and middle classes and automatically transfers the loot to the ultra wealthy. In effect, a low tax Laissez Faire system automatically and handsomely rewards those already ultra rich which simultaneously (and also automatically) penalizes the poor. How does it work?

First, since the ultra wealthy own most of the national investment wealth, most of corporate profits and other investment income goes to them automatically. Note that the ultra wealthy, via our political system, have instructed the Congress to take it easy on investment income, with ultra-low or even zero tax rates on such income. Unrealized capital gains are not taxed at all, and some bond interest is not taxed. Corporations are famous for evading taxes they supposedly owe (legal evasion of course!). Some of the largest and most profitable corporations have managed to pay very low or even zero tax in recent years. At the same time, a wage earner (with little or no investment income), has his (or her) entire income subjected to a significant "pay roll tax". Most corporate income goes to the ultra wealthy because the ultra wealthy own most of the investment property. The after tax income is re-invested, giving the owner an even larger share in the next time period. Note that there is no upper limit to the resulting accumulations of wealth.

The other method is via large salaries: ultra wealthy and influential business owners will award the most lucrative jobs to themselves, and will (of course) use their "influence" to make the salaries as high as the companies can afford. For example, at this point in time, an average company CEO receives about $11 million annually in salary and benefits (ABC news, 7-3-2011). And these well paid CEOs make sure that the company workers are paid as little as possible: currently an average industrial worker receives about $40,000 annually in wages (same ABC news reference).

With a current GDP running at an annual rate of about $15 trillion (including capital replacement cost of about $2 trillion), and with approximately 117 million households out there, the average share of GDP per household works out to approximately $110,000. per annum after capital replacement. (This is not meant to imply that all household incomes should be equal; it is just to point out that, on average, we are still a rather prosperous nation, even in the middle of a severe recession.)

The result is a build up (over many years) of a very high concentration of wealth (and therefore also income) in a few of our wealthiest households. The numbers constantly change, but the overall problem remains stubbornly in place through good times and bad. As observed in recent years, the results are as follows:

■ Share of investment wealth owned by wealthiest 10% of households:
> Over 80%.

■ Share of investment wealth owned by wealthiest 1% of households:
> Over 40%.

■ Annual Income of poorest household:
> About zero.

■ Annual Income of poorest 5% of households:
> Less than $10,000.

■ Annual Income of poorest 25% of households:
> Less than $30,000.

■ Annual Income of 50th percentile household:
> About $50,000.

■ Annual Income of 90th percentile household:
> About $110,000.

■ Annual Income of 99th percentile household:
> About $400,000.

■ Annual Income of 100th percentile household:
> Unknown, but known to be in the $Billions.

If you don't see it immediately, integrating the available data shows conclusively that the richest few percent, and especially the richest one percent of the households, "capture" such a large share of the total national income (of about $15 trillion) that they can live opulent life styles, if they wish, and still have most of their large incomes left over. That richest 1% is intent on mostly reinvesting their huge incomes so that they will have an even larger share next year. The inevitable result, which happens over and over and over again, is that retail sales falter from lack of "economic" demand (the workers don't have enough total income to buy the available finished products). Production is cut back, workers are laid off, and of course the "economic" demand then becomes even less: **recession,** or worse. The "recovery" typically leaves a few percent of the population on the economic sidelines: chronically unemployed or under employed.

Note that the average CEO (about $11 million annual income) has the potential to become an ultra wealthy multi-millionaire in just one year, though he (or she), of course, was probably already a multi-millionaire before he (or she) became a CEO. Also, there is some upward mobility. Note that a super sports star or entertainer (football, basketball, baseball, TV, movies, etc.) can become a multi-millionaire in just one season if he (or she) is just a little bit careful with his (or her) spending. Even congressmen (or congresswomen) can evolve into multi-millionaires if they play their cards right (books, speeches, "sweetheart" business deals). Small wonder that more than a few congress people seem to value the interests of the ultra wealthy over the interests of the workers. A large number of these congressmen (or congresswomen) are ultra wealthy themselves. In fact, more than a few were ultra wealthy even before they ran for congress: being famous and/or beautiful can attract votes whatever your political views. "The rich get richer and the poor get poorer", is not just a joke: it is happening continuously. The poor are also getting to be more numerous.

Is there any way to fix this horrendous problem? Yes. Many people have figured this all out, and some of them have been working to try to enlighten the voters (mostly without success). Check the views of Robert Reich on robertreich.org. Or keep reading this booklet.

* * *

The Business Cycle

A "boom" period sows the seeds of it's own destruction by a number of real and psychological factors:

(1) Almost everyone gets over optimistic, from the poorest car or home buyer to the wealthiest banker. In the absence of effective regulations and controls, many over extend themselves financially. In some cases, there may be an actual excess of federal taxes over expenditures. Instead of paying off some of the national debt, Congress typically reacts to fuel the boom by lowering taxes. We have developed a national attitude that responds to this irresponsible action (lowering taxes) by applauding. Almost everyone optimistically assumes that the boom is going to last forever, in spite of our history that booms have always ended in a recession or depression.

(2)   The operation of "Laissez Faire Capitalism" automatically further enriches the wealthy few, at the expense of almost everybody else: the "poor" and middle classes. This happens automatically because a small percentage of the population owns most of the "investment wealth" and therefore captures most of the investment income. This small group of wealthy are also in a position to demand and get astronomical salaries in addition to their investment income. The rich get richer, everybody else struggles to hold their own, and the very poor actually get poorer.

(3)   At some point, the poor and middle classes lose their ability to cope with the situation by such strategies as multiple jobs per household, and buying things on credit. They necessarily begin to buy less, resulting in sluggish demand for goods and services. Production bosses notice the reduction in demand, and lower production (laying off a few ordinary workers, further lowering demand). A downward spiral develops into a recession or perhaps even a "depression".

(4)   The breakdown typically happens fairly quickly, and, even though it is a common occurrence, having happened repeatedly in the past, it seems to almost always catch almost everybody in a disbelieving surprise. Recovery is likely to be slow and painful, involving bankruptcies, foreclosures, loss of wealth, and some actual starving and freezing among the very poor. Official unemployment figures peak up, and may not fully recover even after the recession is officially declared to be "over".

(5)   As pointed out in the above paragraphs, this sort of undesired business cycle is inevitable in our traditional, "conservative", low tax, low regulation, "rugged individualist", Laissez Faire type of Capitalism. That this is true can be confirmed by merely reviewing our financial history.

(6)   Can anything be done about this? A true Conservative will, of course, say no. To him (or her) it is just an inevitable and normal part of business. It always recovers after a while, they say.

Unfortunate that some of the poorest people have to starve and freeze every time, but thats just the way things are.

(7)   A more careful analysis of the history leads to different conclusions. The great depression of the 1930s, for example, showed no sign of complete recovery until the onset of WWII provided the impetus and the conditions needed to snap out of the depression. Although all of the conditions for prosperity were not met in the WWII and post WWII experience, enough conditions were satisfied (e.g., relatively high progressive personal income tax, social security, unemployment payments, welfare) to provide a period of ***relative prosperity*** which lasted for almost 35 years before some of the safeguards started to be dismantled and things started to fail again.

(8)   The secrets of prosperity, as pointed out and explained in other essays and even in books, include high progressive taxation ala WWII for personal income, corporate profits, large gifts and bequests, and estates; massive federal government stimulus projects (e.g., upgrade infrastructure and public transportation and power generation); and simultaneously pay off the national debt and never borrow again. An engineer can easily point out how this could be made to be a self correcting system with no more recessions or depressions. This would have to be a never ending policy to be effective and self correcting: i.e., permanent high progressive taxes, permanent federal stimulus programs (such as

universal health care and social security coupled with continuous public infrastructure repair and upgrade).

***

Correlations

The economic history of the past hundred years shows that:

(1) The ideology of "reagonomics" (minimal federal taxation coupled with little or no governmental services) naturally and automatically enriches only the already rich; impoverishes almost everyone else; and leads to an inevitable depression. And

(2)That the opposite ideology (very high progressive taxation coupled with massive federal stimulus spending) led to the most prosperous period our country has ever known (about 1940 to about 1965).

The graphs of Figures 1 and 2 cover approximately the last hundred years, ending in the year 2010.

Figure 1 shows the percentage of national "money income" captured by the wealthiest 10% of us since 1917. This graph is taken from an article by Emmanuel Saez: Summary for the broader public "Striking it Richer: The Evolution of Top Incomes in the United States", updated March 2012), which in turn is based on an article by Piketty & Saez ("Income Inequality in the United States, 1913-1998" with Thomas Piketty, Quarterly Journal of Economics, 118(1), 2003, 1-39). For the original articles, see the URL http://elsa.berkeley.edu/~saez/

Figure 2 is a graph I plotted showing a variety of economic data for the past hundred years. The key data is the curve of maximum income tax rate on the maximum tax bracket. This curve clearly shows when one or the other of the two ideologies (Reagonomics, or high taxation with federal stimulus) was dominant, and indicates the transition periods. The "income capture" curve of Fig. 1 (including realized capital gains) is also shown as the "Top Decile Share" curve of Fig. 2.

Figure 4 (shown in section "C" of chapter 5, "Dysfunctional USA Politics") illustrates the ridiculous concentration of income in the wealthiest one percent of the USA households. The distribution is skewed so badly that the poorest few percent of households have no significant income at the same time that the very wealthiest households have literally billions of dollars of annual after tax income. Careful analysis of the other two figures (Fig 1 and Fig 2) shows that this extreme maldistribution is an automatic result of the normal operation of Laissez Faire Capitalism.

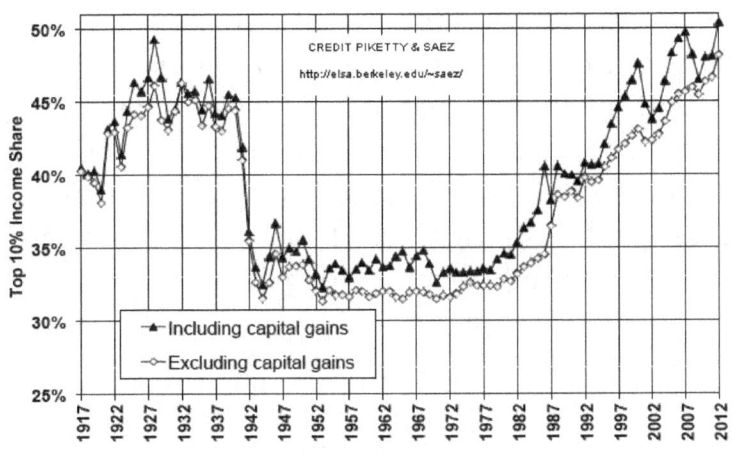

FIGURE 1
The Top Decile Income Share, 1917-2012

Starting with Figure 1 (or the "Top Decile Share" curve of Fig. 2), note that the first data point in 1917 showed that the wealthiest 10% of us was "capturing" about 40% of the national "money income" in 1917. This value didn't change very much for a few years (probably an effect from WWI). Then, correlating with the low tax rates of the roaring 1920s, it starts a "noisy" (volatile) climb to a value near 50% capture of national money income in 1928. This peak signaled the start of system instability, culminating in the stock market crash of 1929 and the start of the "Great Depression", which constituted the first documented catastrophic failure of Reagonomics, even before Reagonomics had a name. At this point, the wealthy "capture" rate drops back to a "noisy" (volatile) value near 45%, where it remains for the rest of the

Great Depression. Looking back at the tax rate curves of Figure 2, the Great Depression period correlates with intermediate tax rates (income and corporate taxes too low to solve the problem), and therefore with inadequate, only partially effective, federal stimulus programs. The Great Depression was "ameliorated", but did not go away. Then, WWII reared its ugly head.

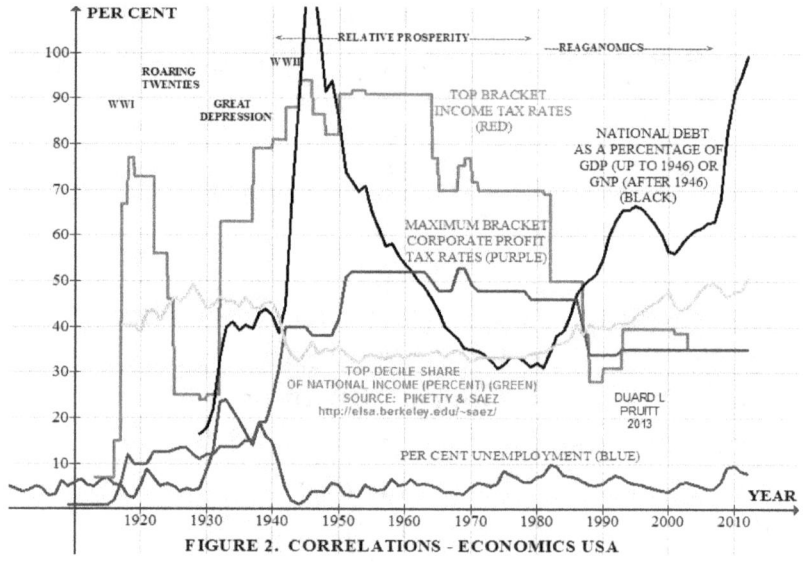

FIGURE 2. CORRELATIONS - ECONOMICS USA

Terrible as this time was, it contained a lesson which we sorely needed, but promptly forgot even before the war was over. In a nutshell, the message was that really massive government stimulus programs (adopted to cope with WWII), coupled with really high progressive taxes, are incompatible with a depression. The depression loses and very quickly disappears. The graphs show the lesson clearly: the "top decile" "capture" of national

18

"money income" fell steeply to a final value of about one-third (about 33%). The unemployment percentage fell to less than 1%. And the "Top Bracket Income Tax Rate" curve shows that the max bracket income tax rate was (bi-partisanly) raised to a high of 94%. High as this was, the corporate (especially) and individual tax rates combined were not high enough to completely stabilize the system: the national debt rose to a value greater than GNP. The resources required to prosecute the war were there, as is proven by the fact that the national debt money was supplied from the income of the countries citizens, primarily the wealthy citizens. <u>Overall score: one short period of massive federal government stimulus resulted in one rip roaring success: Great Depression banished, and a relatively prosperous USA for more than a quarter of a century.</u>

Please note that the USA was not the only country to experience this phenomenon. The Great Depression was a world wide depression, which a number of other countries escaped in the same way.

First, Japan wasn't badly effected by the Great Depression, because Japan was in war mode all of the time. Italy recovered by going to a dictatorship: Mussolini "made the trains run on time", among other things. (He also had a war, incorporating Ethiopia into the Italian Empire). Germany promoted Hitler to dictator, and he quickly started building things like the autobahn (and also secretly preparing for war). As I have noted somewhere else, these "miraculous" recoveries from a deep depression were at least a part of the reason that Mussolini and Hitler were initially very popular in their respective countries. Sure enough, none of the western democracies fully recovered until they were finally fully involved in the war.

After WWII, there was a brief move to reduce the income tax rates, but they were returned to 91% maximum in 1950 (Korean War). The "upper 10%" wealthy segment "income capture" stabilized around a value of about one third. The large WWII national debt was being sharply reduced for about 20 years. Under both Democratic and Republican Administrations, the max bracket income tax rate was kept above 90% (a peak of 92% under the Eisenhower Administration). This was a "relatively prosperous" period, which may be unique in our economic history.

Then in 1964-1965 the Johnson administration lowered the income tax rates sharply in two stages. Reduction of the national debt became slower, and then ground to a halt in the mid 1970s.

1980 was a tipping point. The Reagan Administration sharply reduced tax rates, which became a very bad habit during the Reagan and Busch Administrations. The national debt immediately started to climb steeply, and it is still climbing, after a brief stabilization during the Clinton Administration. The percentage of "money income" captured by the upper decile started a steady rise in about 1980, reaching a bad, noisy, value near 50% in 2007, similar to the noisy 1928 peak. And, just like in 1929, economic collapse hit in 2008, <u>completing a second documented catastrophic failure of "Reaganomics" (Laissez Faire Capitalism).</u> As of 2012, although the "Great" Recession has been officially declared to be over, we are in reality still in this recession period, known by some economists as "The Great Recession".

<u>And the prime correlations we observe are:</u>

(1) When the federal tax rates are low enough (as in the 1920s and in the 1980 to 2010 time periods), a Depression can be expected. The timing of the depression is uncertain, but the factors to cause it are in place. The 2008 "Great Recession" took several times as long to set up as the 1929 "Great Depression" for several observable reasons. These included the fact that we were closer to the depression in 1920 (upper decile "money income capture" was already about 40% in 1920). Also there were no public safety nets in place in 1920 to 1930. By contrast, in the latter period (1980 to 2010) we started from an upper decile "money income capture" of about 33% (farther to go for instability), and we had some social security payments, some medicare payments, and some unemployment payments to provide a little spending demand and thus slow the process down.

(2) When the federal tax rates are high enough

(similar to WWII levels), and the federal
spending stimulus is also high enough (as in
the 1940 to 1946 period) full employment and
prosperity either exist or can be expected to
occur quickly.

(3) Given these obvious insights, why in the
world do about 50% of us consistently vote
for those policies that cause widespread
poverty, rather than the more desirable
widespread prosperity? (In our Congress, a
majority of greater than 60% is required in
the Senate to get anything done).

***

Wealth & Income (mal)Distribution in the USA

Figure 3 below, WEALTH & ANNUAL INCOME DISTRIBUTION (USA), clearly shows our national economic problem with just a minimum of study.

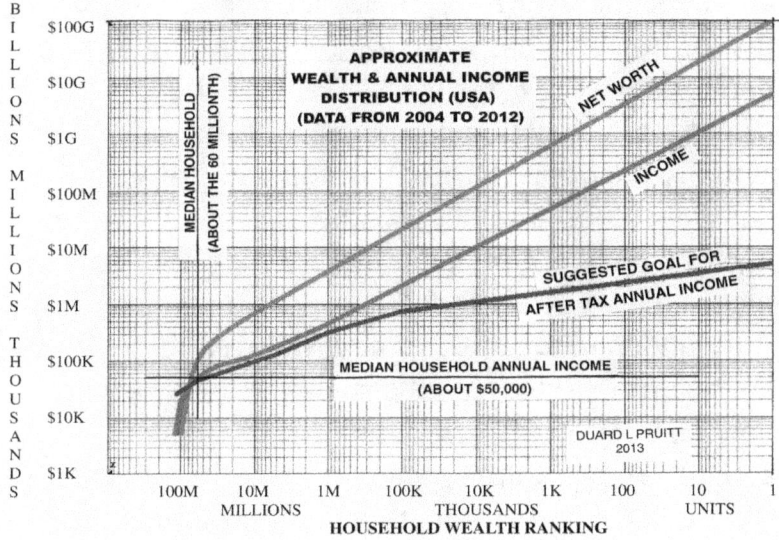

FIG 3. WEALTH AND INCOME DISTRIBUTION IN THE USA

The right hand 2/3 of the chart shows that about one percent of the households (about 1.2 million households) have a household net worth of about three million dollars or more, ranging up to about sixty billion dollars per household. The annual income (before taxes) of this top one percent ranges from about 400 thousand dollars to several billion dollars per household. This is the portion of the population that lives a rather luxurious life style (compared to most of the remaining 99%), and still has funds left over to invest. With very few exceptions, this group grows richer every year.

23

Over time, this group acquires ownership over a larger and larger portion of the US economy. The effect varies over this 1% group: at the low end, the growth may be relatively modest, but as we approach the high end of the range, the growth becomes a Biblical flood. Reflect that, over the past 40 years, the ***average*** growth rate per year of the top two billionaires has been ***greater than one billion dollars per year after taxes!*** Finally, there is no limit to this growth, and the current tax codes actually encourages this astronomical growth: the tax rates on investment income are actually lower than the rates on low paid worker's wages. This is the trickle up effect that this top 1% must certainly fully understand, and yet they (the wealthiest 1%) are determined to keep the rules just like they are now, thank you. (Correction: the top 1% are actually engaged in a policy of austerity: further reduce taxes and eliminate federal programs such as social security and medicare, so that their wealth capture rates will actually increase). Note that the national debt doesn't really bother the wealthy segment; they own most of it themselves, and thus collect most of the interest paid on the debt by the national government.

By contrast, the households in the lower portion of the wealth curve, especially those at or below the median level (about the 60,000,000[th] household), have been losing ground the past 40 years or so. With a significant and apparently permanent unemployment rate since just after WWII, wages are ***small***. No bargaining power for the wage earner: he (or she) has to just take the small wage that is offered. Since capitalism is a zero sum game, those small wages automatically equate to higher profits for the owners, which will, of course, be taxed primarily at the low rates for investment income. As the factories modernize and automate, fewer workers are required, making the high unemployment rate a chronic problem. The profits from the automated factories all go to the owners and the unemployed workers are out of luck. You can understand why the wealthiest 1% believes that all of this is fine and dandy.

The recurrent problem is that capitalism _**is**_ a zero sum game: i.e., for every wealthy household that receives tens, hundreds, or even thousands of times an average share of income, there must be even more wage earner households with a fraction (in many cases even a small fraction) of a share. The wage squeezed workers will resort to actions such as multiple wage earners per household and buying goods on credit. Multiple jobs per household puts abnormal stress on the family, and buying on credit is a self defeating policy: the money wasted on interest reduces the ability to buy the goods for sale. The normal result is an intolerable buildup of household debt, eventually ending in enforced reduction in buying and a resulting recession or depression. As "conservatives" may point out, after some period of "hard times" the recession will ease up, except that the high unemployment rate has been a chronic and permanent feature of our economy since just after WWII. If you look carefully, the wealthy segment may have recovered from a recession, but a portion of the citizenry has fallen into a chronic and apparently permanent status of unemployment or underemployment.

***

"The Moral Equivalent of War"
(Quote used by Jimmy Carter)

The United States, and the World, is grappling with the worst problems ever to confront a civilization. Serious over population strains our natural resources, which are running out, and causing the environment to deteriorate. Oil, the base of our global economy, is about half used up world wide, and the second half will disappear much faster than the first half because global demand just keeps rising. Burning our fossil fuels is causing the Earths temperature to increase significantly, leading to climate change, ocean level rise, and species die offs (some people still deny that this is happening, but scientists agree that the evidence is overwhelming). Our global financial systems (mostly Laissez Faire Capitalism), automatically and naturally enrich a very small percentage of the population, and just as automatically penalizes almost everyone else, with an increasing percentage of impoverished unemployed and underemployed world wide, including the United States.

Is there any way to halt the slide into chaos? Let us consider the financial system first, since just about all else hinges on keeping as much of the population as possible fed, housed, and clothed.

(1) Examine the history of our "Great Depression" and WWII. After almost a decade of wrestling with the Great Depression without really solving the problem, the onset of WWII stopped the depression

in its tracks very quickly and completely. We failed miserably to analyze why at the time, but about 70 years of history and financial experience has provided some hind sight which makes it clear what happened. Briefly, the key was putting everybody back to work (in the war effort in the case of WWII), and mostly paying for the effort by raising the personal income tax to high rates for the top brackets of a progressive structure.

(2) As noted by someone else in his memoirs, a good question is why were we unable to accomplish this feat in peace time, but did it very quickly in the pursuit of a destructive war?

(3) And the answer of course, using 70 years of 20-20 hindsight, is that we could have abolished the depression in peace time, but we didn't because of a lack of political will. Most voters were unable to understand the problems, resulting in disagreements, opposition, indecision, and lack of adequate appropriate action. Then WWII came along and supplied the impetus to do what needed to be done: (a) Massive federal government stimulus programs put everybody back to work, and (b) Pay for the effort with very high and very progressive personal income taxes. We still have that problem today (2011). In the midst of global turmoil, the United States is concentrating on reducing personal income tax rates to as near zero as possible, while the corporations use loopholes and special provisions to avoid paying any significant corporate tax. At the same time, instead of putting people back to work,

we are proposing to trash social security and medicare and are laying off teachers and public servants, on the grounds that there is no money to pay the bills. Obviously, we didn't learn the lessons supplied by WWII.

(4) The global crisis that we are now facing requires the equivalent of a "PEACE TIME WAR EFFORT" if we are to have any chance of terminating the financial crisis and saving our planet. In short, this could be:

"THE MORAL EQUIVALENT OF WAR"

I know, this isn't my quote. I got it from a famous President (Jimmy Carter), who suggested such an approach to the oil problem a few decades ago. We don't have to actually go to war, we could make peace time infrastructure instead of war materials, and we should not actually "overspend". We should actually start repaying the national debt as a part of the effort.

Fortuitously, the actions required to stop the looming depression can fit right in with minimizing the effects of global warming and overpopulation. Suitable stimulus programs could include border patrol duty, electrifying the national railway system, developing small electrical automobiles for short range use, converting our electricity generating system into a post oil age "green" system, renewing our aging infrastructure in general, upgrading our national parks, and a probably near endless list of useful projects.

***

Dysfunctional USA Politics

We have evolved to have two major political parties. A third party emerges now and then, but always seems to fade away with no lasting impression. Each party tends to take a stand on a number of presumably unrelated issues, and these positions have somehow been divided in such a way that, year in and year out, the two parties tend to share national governmental positions more or less 50-50: evenly divided.

Congressional rules (e.g., Senate filibuster) have evolved in such a way that this even division is guaranteed to cause a stalemate on any controversial legislation: a "super majority" being required in the Senate to pass such legislation.

A. THE MOST IMPORTANT ISSUE!:

This might all be a "so what" except that there is one extremely important issue, with radically opposite interests at stake, where a tiny minority has been consistently able to enforce its viewpoint at the expense of the vast majority (the tail wags the dog). The issue is financial policy: the rules for our national economy. The winning policies have tended to be low tax rates, especially for the wealthy, and minimal regulations on banks, mortgage institutions, and business in general. What seems to be fully understood by only a tiny segment of our population (primarily some university economics professors) is that, over a period of time, these policies automatically lead to a nations wealth, and therefore also its income, being concentrated in a very small percentage of the population, causing financial disruptions which lead to recessions and depressions, unemployment, underemployment, and an increasingly weaker, less wealthy, nation. In short, over a period of years, the investment wealth of the society automatically moves upward to the wealthy segment who comprise at most a few percent of the population. The fact that we have many recessions and depressions should be all the proof necessary to show that there is something seriously wrong with our financial system.

"Conservatives" will of course scoff at this thought, but the truth is that the economic history of our country (USA) over the last hundred years conclusively proves that the above statements are true. You just have to chart the figures in the appropriate historical economic records and study them carefully. More than one person has done just that in the last few years. The "ROARING 1920s", the "Great Depression", and WWII combined at just the perfect timing to clearly show the cause of a "Great Depression" and also what finally ended "The Great Depression": namely the national government taxation and spending policies adopted to cope with WWII. And after WWII the fact that the marginal tax rate was left high enough (by both Republican and Democratic administrations) to keep the economy *relatively* stable and prosperous until the ill advised tax cuts of the 1980s and beyond. And, yes, a particular curve plotted by Piketty and

Saez (percentage of money income "captured" by the wealthiest 10%) starts to climb out of bounds by the mid 1980s and keeps going up until it achieves a very bad level by 2007, approximately repeating what the same data had shown in the 1920s. It is no accident that a "Great Depression" began in late 1929, and a corresponding "Great Recession" began in 2008. The timing may be somewhat accidental, but both events were made inevitable by our country's financial policies: minimal taxation and minimal regulations. Jobs are lost, households slip into poverty, and almost everyone has to worry that their jobs may be the next to get the ax, except of course that wealthiest one percent (or less) who own enough financial wealth to be immune to depressions and recessions.

The extremely wealthy comprise no more than ½% to 1% of the population, though the wealth curve is, of course, continuous with no obvious "break" points. If you define the ultra wealthy as those with enough investment wealth and therefore investment income to be able to cope with any conceivable catastrophe, such as complete loss of job or an expensive, long term, incapacitating medical problem (which could lead to a complete loss of job), then ½% is maybe the right number. Don't dismiss the argument because of the small numbers: that wealthiest 1% owns over 40% of the USA investment wealth. Below this level, it may be that a 95th percentile household (about $150,000 annual income and about $900,000 net worth) could perhaps buy insurance to cover such catastrophes, although a long term loss of job could limit ability to buy insurance after the initial shock. A 90th percentile household (about $110,000 annual income and about $700,000 net worth) could have a little more trouble. And an 80th percentile household (about $100,000 annual income and about $350,000 net worth) would be even less able to cope with an extended illness. Note, that in these "lower" percentile households, the net worth figure can be mostly the equity in the home, which is not investment wealth and does not generate any investment income. One could easily argue that the 80th, or 90th, or even 95th percentile households have more in common with the median household and below (where the cost of effective health insurance is clearly out of an individual household's reach) than with the super wealthy elite.

But although the majority of our households are unable to afford effective health insurance, it is well within the capabilities of the entire country, as can be easily seen by comparing two figures: the gross national product (which basically equals gross national income) and the national cost of complete health care. The annual GNP has been almost $15 trillion recently, and a recent figure for annual total national health care was about $2.5 trillion. Thus, total health care cost is about one-sixth of Gross national income. A most significant figure, but far from overwhelming. The super wealth of the wealthiest ½% is super enough to make the entire nation easily able to afford something (health care) which the poorest 60% to 80% cannot handle as individual households. Yes, we should endeavor to emulate all other civilized countries and reduce this cost. Our health care is the costliest in the world, and, contrary to "conservative" rhetoric, is not the worlds best. Some other countries have superior life expectancy and infant mortality, to name just two categories of excellence. But, even with costs as they now are, we could, as a united country, easily afford it. What is needed is the political will to do it.

B. WHAT IS THE BLOCKING MECHANISM?

The stumbling block is that a general lack of understanding of the problem, and sometimes a preoccupation with other (lesser???) issues, has led to forfeiting control of our financial policy to that elite 1% or so of extremely wealthy, who have few interests in common with the rest of us. Minimal taxation fits their attitudes exactly. Their wealth is sufficient that they have no need for the public services that are vital to most of the rest of us. They can "ride out" recessions and depressions without any deprivations and their fortunes will resume the upward trend with the next boom period. Their investment incomes are more than adequate to sustain their lavish lifestyles, and the large surpluses are used to buy up an even larger share of the national wealth.

Who are these extremely wealthy, any way, and doesn't "upward mobility" continually replace them with new people? This process has been going on for thousands of years, albeit with at least a partial reset now and then (for example, I suspect that the sacking of Rome, or the Norman conquest of England, led to the financial ruin of a few rich guys). In our case, the colonists from England were unequal from the moment they stepped ashore. A chosen few had already received large land grants from the Crown. A few others were already wealthy from some English fortune. A lot of our currently wealthy no doubt are just the current beneficiaries of large family fortunes: e.g., Roosevelts, Byrds, Rockefellers, Cabots, and Lodges. As for upward mobility, with very, very, few exceptions we are talking about people who at least had an excellent higher education supplied by affluent parents. Most people aspire to winning the lottery to make it big, but there is only one winner for many millions of ticket buyers. A commonly recognized way is to be either a top entertainer (e.g., a movie star) or a top athlete. The lucky ones can command a salary of up to $20 million or more, enough to live like a king and still join that wealthiest percent almost from their first successful year. Again, only a few successes from millions of aspirants. Politicians also are prime candidates. A little harder for a politician, perhaps, but successful ones can climb that ladder after a couple of decades of successful politicking (speeches, books, "sweetheart" business deals). Think of that: the representatives and senators that you elect to represent you have a chance of being your natural financial enemies! (They should excuse themselves from voting on taxation and budgetary matters because of conflict of interest!). And once one has built up an investment wealth of a few dozen millions (that top ½ %), merely prudent investment practices are guaranteed to keep your fortune growing ad infinitum.

C. APPROXIMATE INCOME DISTRIBUTION IN THE USA

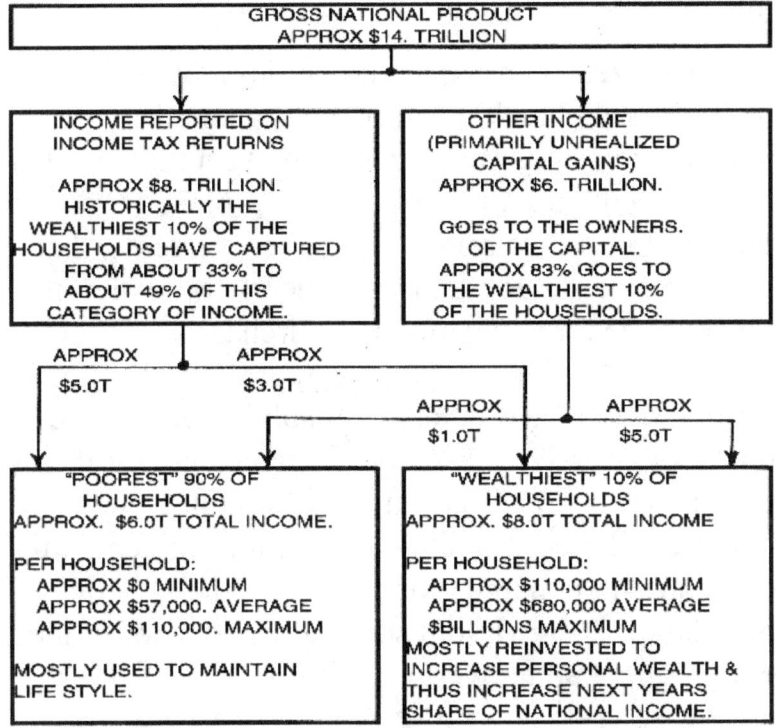

Figure 4. Approximate USA Income Distribution ca 2010

Figure 4 shows the approximate division of United States income between the "poorest" 90% and the "wealthiest" 10% of the population, ca 2010. Wealth and resulting income is highly concentrated among the wealthiest 10% (especially the wealthiest

1%) because the wealthiest owners, having more income than is required to live an opulent lifestyle, inevitably invest and reinvest the surplus. Thus, they gradually and automatically, over the years, acquire a higher and higher share of the national economy. If the local economy is too weak, they will gladly send their investments overseas. Why is this lop sided distribution bad?

The basic reason has been pointed out by Robert Reich ("Aftershock") and others. A small percentage of high income earners "capture" such a high percentage of national income, most of which they will invest or reinvest (maybe overseas), that the remaining income to the general population is nowhere near large enough to purchase all of the goods and services that the economy is capable of turning out. The predictable result is business cut back and layoffs. A significant percentage of the population becomes chronically unemployed or under employed. Capitalism responds to economic demand: no demand, no response. The general population is slowly but surely pushed toward under employment and poverty.

D. THIS IS A DEMOCRACY – WHY DON'T WE FIX IT?

In theory, it should be easily fixed. The Great Depression and our response to WWII clearly showed the mechanism for a fix. Part of the fix was a very high, very progressive, income tax with no exceptions allowed: all income, including investment income, to be taxed the same. In WWII

(1944) the highest bracket tax rate was 94%. This tax policy, of course, interrupts the sequence of events wherein the lion's share of the country's income goes to the wealthy and sticks there, instead of being used to stimulate the economy. The second part of the fix is to use the funds obtained from this progressive taxation to put the unemployed and underemployed back to useful work. In WWII the impetus was to make the people soldiers, sailors, and war workers, and the combination of fixes ended the Great Depression very quickly. Note that the very high taxes imposed did not hinder recovery at all, contrary to current political dogma. We don't need wartime stuff, but there is no end to needed public projects such as national infrastructure which has been rotting away under our current dysfunctional system. We could upgrade Amtrak to become a national high speed network just in time to overcome transportation difficulties from the coming oil shortage. We could upgrade our energy generation plants for green operation and better reliability. And pay off the national debt. Public services such as social security and health care need to be upgraded.

Now, back to Earth. It seems that the political climate (ca 2011) almost guarantees failure. The leadership of our new house of representatives majority is focused on tax reduction and elimination of public services. The history outlined above shows that these are policies which are guaranteed to make our problems worse over a few years.

We need a new political party, or at least a re-dedication of a current party (Progressive Republocrats???), designed to lead and educate the voters on what is needed to fix our dysfunctional economic system for the benefit of *everyone*, not just the wealthiest ½%. The way our national legislature is constituted, this could take as much as six years (in the Senate) to completely turn around, even after the voting public becomes aware of the nature of the problem, and is convinced to vote for reform. Note that a "super majority" is required to achieve reform: at least 70% of us must vote for reform to make it happen. Since at least 90% of us are poorly treated by the current system, one might think that obtaining a 70% majority would be a breeze. Unfortunately, this may not be the case. Some voters may neglect or refuse to examine the evidence, others will just refuse to believe the documented history, and a small percentage has no interest in fixing the system, even though they may fully understand what is happening. And that tiny percentage, with their vast wealth, will continue to flood the news media with misleading and even false propaganda.

***

Economic Profit

As noted previously, the wealthiest 10% of our households receive most of the nations investment income because the wealthiest 10% own most of the nations investment wealth.

To survive, businesses must operate with a "positive" economic profit. If a business operates at an "economic loss" for any length of time, it may go bankrupt. A zero profit could theoretically be sustained, but in practice an exact zero profit is practically impossible to achieve. In practice, the profit will be either positive or negative, where negative means losses and eventual bankruptcy.

"Economic" profit is defined as the excess of gross sales over gross expenses, where the expenses include replacement of used up capital and the wages and salaries of all of the employees including the owners. I believe that economists have long understood that in the long run and with a stable competitive economy, economic profit will be **_zero_**, because in a free system if there was a "positive" economic profit more firms would be expected to engage in whatever activity was returning that profit, thus increasing supply of that product and causing a product price reduction until the economic profit goes to zero.

In case you haven't already noticed it, there is the distinct possibility of a squeeze on the salaries of the owners, if they are awarding themselves salaries in excess of a "normal" salary (the salary they could obtain by applying their skills at a firm they did not own). In the face of ultimate long run competition their firm will be forced by the lowering of product prices to lower their (the owners) salaries to the "normal" value to avoid a loss.

This brings up the concept of "normal" profits. where the profit is considered to be the amount that the owner or owners are collecting as salaries, and where these amounts may be in agreement with a "normal" value. This is probably the understanding at most small businesses such as a single owner farm or a single owner business in general. The owner may take as his (or her) salary all that is left over from the total receipts after all of the expenses have been paid, what ever that sum is. You can see that a single owner business may be able to break the rule that you can't operate in the face of "economic losses" by the owner just accepting whatever "profit" is left over, even if it is smaller than what would be considered a "normal profit".

So how do large firms in the USA (and around the world) consistently pay their executives enormous sums, clearly greater than any possible "normal" value, and yet still manage to turn out enormous profits? ABC news reported (on July 3rd, 2011) that CEOs in the United States had *average* salaries plus bonuses of about $11 million last year, or an average of about 275 times the average wage of an industrial worker. It appears that our large corporations have been able to avoid the problem of zero profit and no more than "normal" compensation that should be caused by normal competition. There must be an element of monopoly at work here. It is difficult to break into a large business where the capital requirements are huge. Brand differentiation and small or large detail differences in the product prevent perfect competition. Also, in the modern world, with weak labor unions, the companies are able to "squeeze" the workers. In the USA the average annual income of an industrial worker (about $40,000. recently, according to the ABC news item reported above) is about 35% of a country wide "average" household income. This figure is a bit low partly because of the influence of the global economy, where most workers in the world at large have even smaller incomes, which acts as a limit on the incomes of USA workers (the companies will "outsource" product manufacture if the workers demand more). Also, large companies can, in effect, even squeeze the income of executives in small companies in other fields where competition may be much more severe. Small business owners may be compelled to accept an income which is less than "normal" in order to stay in business. If it is hard to see how this relates to the larger companies larger profits, just reflect on the fact that the ability of the larger companies to charge higher prices for their products (which is where their excess profits come from) means that the public who buy those products will necessarily have less money left to buy the products where the competition is keener. The fact that the weak economy has a large percentage of unemployed and an even larger percentage of underemployed workers enhances the ability of the companies (large and small) to minimize workers wages. In a low tax rate, low public services environment, all of these facts not only lock in a weak economy, they contribute to the economy gradually getting ever weaker as time goes on.

Note that our annual economic activity consists of many billions of transactions, each involving a seller and a buyer. It may be a worker selling his services to an employer, or a shopper buying some item in a mall, or any one of many billions of transactions. In each transaction, the buyer incurs an expense, and the seller receives some money called a receipt, and of course in each individual case the receipt equals the expense. You don't have to be a rocket scientist to figure out that the total annual receipts equals the total annual expenses. It is a zero sum game: no overall economic profit. It is no secret, however, that almost all large corporations will turn in a positive economic profit for the year. That is the fuel that keeps the stock market running. Over some number of transactions, economic gains can occur, and, of course, for every gain there must be a loss somewhere else. But since the overall game *is* a zero sum affair, where do those profits come from? We answered that question in the above paragraphs. It should come as no surprise that the poor and middle classes are the big losers in the economic game of LAISSEZ FAIRE CAPITALISM.

Conservatives will argue forever that Laissez Faire Capitalism is a perfect system, and that these flaws, insofar as they may exist, are the fault of the lazy workers, not a characteristic of the system. But a careful and critical study of our economic history, with frequent recessions and depressions, contains the proof that Laissez Faire Capitalism is unstable and unfair. The system harbors a "trickle up" effect, wherein the country's wealth automatically moves away from the poor and middle classes and up to the ultra wealthy where it sticks. The Great Depression resulted from the low tax rates and minimal business regulations of the 1920s. The Great Depression was ended by the high tax rates, full employment, and huge federal stimulus programs brought on by our response to World War II. The current ailing economy developed more slowly than the Great Depression, starting in the 1970s, and getting much worse through the 1980s and 1990s. But the root causes are the same: lower and lower tax rates and dismantling of regulations. Note that, under low tax rate policy, our national debt started to increase rapidly in the early 1980s and is still going up rapidly (except for a relatively stable period between about 1993 and about 2001). The data and analyses that prove these assertions are the subject of other essays, and are contained in available books and booklets. Refer to ISBN 1463567499 or ISBN 978-1461117186. Or checkout http://duardlpruitt.blog.com

Government Shutdown

Which party is responsible for the recent shutdown? Both? Neither?

Actually, it is another flaw in our constitution. note that our original constitution had a total of VII articles, and we have so far seen fit to add XXVII amendments. The problem of government shutdown shows that it is still flawed. Something that should never even be allowed to be considered has happened. Given that laissez faire capitalism has a major flaw of its own (automatic, astronomical, and continuing without limit, concentration of the nations wealth to less than 1% of our population, which makes laissez faire capitalism be neither fair nor stable), how about a couple of long overdue constitutional amendments?

AMENDMENT XX???

THE UNITED STATES FEDERAL GOVERNMENT SHALL NEVER "SHUT DOWN" OR REDUCE OPERATIONS FOR ANY REASON, INCLUDING "LACK OF FUNDS". IN CASE OF A TEMPORARY FUND SHORTAGE, THE FEDERAL RESERVE BANK SHALL EXPAND THE NATIONAL MONEY SUPPLY AS NECESSARY TO KEEP THE GOVERNMENT FULLY OPERATIONAL. THE FEDERAL GOVERNMENT SHALL NEVER AGAIN "BORROW" FROM ANY SOURCE, NEITHER

PRIVATE CITIZENS OF ANY COUNTRY, NOR FOREIGN GOVERNMENTS, NOR ANY OTHER SOURCE. THE COUNTRY SHALL ALWAYS CONTINUE TO FULLY OPERATE IN ACCORDANCE WITH CURRENTLY APPLICABLE LAWS UNTIL SUCH TIME AS THE CONGRESS AND THE PRESIDENT ENACT NEW OR REPLACEMENT LAWS AND SIGN THEM INTO EFFECT. IT IS THE RESPONSIBILITY OF THE CONGRESS AND THE PRESIDENT TO PROVIDE INTERNAL REVENUE LAWS WHICH FULLY FUND THE GOVERNMENTS LEGAL OPERATIONS AT ALL TIMES.

AMENDMENT XX????

TO FUND THE OPERATION OF THE UNITED STATES FEDERAL GOVERNMENT, THE CONGRESS SHALL PROVIDE APPROPRIATE REVENUE BILLS INCLUDING:

[A]   A PERSONAL INCOME TAX LAW WHICH PROVIDES A PROGRESSIVE STRUCTURE WHICH INCLUDES (1) A "PAYROLL" TAX OF AT LEAST 10%, TO FUND SOCIAL SECURITY, WHICH SHALL BE LEVIED ON TOTAL GROSS PERSONAL INCOME OF ALL KINDS AND CATEGORIES; (2) A PROVISION THAT ALL TAXABLE INCOME IN EXCESS OF FIVE MILLION DOLLARS SHALL BE TAXED AT A MARGINAL RATE OF AT LEAST 95%,

WHETHER THE DECLARATION IS FOR A
SINGLE TAXPAYER, MARRIED COUPLE
FILING JOINTLY, OR HEAD OF HOUSEHOLD;
(3) TAX RATES TO BE APPLICABLE TO THE
SUM OF ALL CATAGORIES OF INCOME,
WHETHER WAGES, SALARIES, INVESTMENT
INCOME OF ALL KINDS (WITH THE SOLE
EXCEPTION OF UNREALIZED CAPITAL
GAINS), GAMBLING, BRIBERY, STEALING,
CHEATING, EXTORTION, AND ANY OTHER
TYPE OF INCOME; (4) ITEMIZED
DEDUCTIONS AND EXEMPTIONS OF ANY
KIND SHALL BE DISALLOWED, EXCEPT
THAT THE AMOUNT OF THE PAYROLL TAX -
PLUS STATE INCOME TAX - PLUS A
SPECIFIED MAXIMUM AMOUNT BY LAW,
INDEPENDENT RETIREMENT ACCOUNT
CONTRIBUTION - PLUS A STANDARD
DEDUCTION OF FIFTEEN THOUSAND
DOLLARS PER TAXPAYER - SHALL BE
ALLOWED.

[B]   GIFT TAX: CONGRESS SHALL PROVIDE
FOR A PROGRESSIVE GIFT TAX WHICH
SHALL PROVIDE A MINIMUM TAX RATE OF
AT LEAST 50% ON THE TAXABLE PORTION
OF GIFTS THAT EXCEEDS $500,000 PER
BENEFICIARY, PER TAX YEAR, PAYABLE BY
THE DONOR. GIFTS AND GIFT TAXES ARE
NOT DEDUCTIBLE FROM TAXABLE INCOME.

[C]   A PROGRESSIVE CORPORATE PROFITS
TAX WHICH SHALL CONTAIN THE

FOLLOWING TAX RATES AS A MINIMUM. THE PORTION OF CORPORATE PROFITS DISTRIBUTED TO THE SHARE OWNERS SHALL NOT BE TAXED TO THE CORPORATION, BUT SHALL BE INCLUDED IN THE SHARE OWNERS PERSONAL INCOME TAX DECLARATIONS. CORPORATE PROFITS RETAINED IN THE COMPANY SHALL BE TAXED AT A BASE RATE OF 50%, EXCEPT THAT THE PORTION OF RETAINED PROFITS EXCEEDING ONE HUNDRED MILLION DOLLARS SHALL BE TAXED AT THE MARGINAL RATE OF 95%. NO EXEMPTIONS OR DEDUCTIONS ARE ALLOWED.

[D]   A PROGRESSIVE ESTATE TAX SHALL CONTAIN THE FOLLOWING PROVISIONS AS A MINIMUM: (1) A DEDUCTION OF TEN MILLION DOLLARS SHALL BE ALLOWED; (2) ESTATE VALUE IN EXCESS OF THE DEDUCTION SHALL BE TAXED AT A RATE OF 70%.

[E]   ALL UNITED STATES CITIZENS AND ALL UNITED STATES CORPORATIONS (OR A BUSINESS BY ANY OTHER NAME) SHALL BE FULLY TAXED PER THE REQUIREMENTS ABOVE. ANY FOREIGN PERSON EITHER RESIDING IN THE UNITED STATES OR EARNING INCOME IN THE UNITED STATES IS SUBJECT TO THE FULL PROVISIONS OF THE TAX LAWS.   INCOME EARNED IN A FOREIGN COUNTRY SHALL BE INCLUDED IN ALL TAX

DECLARATIONS, EITHER BY A CITIZEN, A
RESIDENT, OR A CORPORATION, EXCEPT
THAT TAXES LEGALLY COLLECTED BY A
FOREIGN COUNTRY MAY BE DEDUCTED
FROM THE FOREIGN DERIVED INCOME.

[F]   IN THE EVENT THAT A CONGRESS AND
PRESIDENT ARE UNABLE TO AGREE ON
INTERNAL REVENUE BILLS, THE PREVIOUS
LEGALLY ENACTED LAWS WILL CONTINUE
IN FULL FORCE AND EFFECT UNTIL A NEW
AGREEMENT IS REACHED. TIME LIMITS ON
REVENUE BILLS ARE NOT ALLOWED, AND
AT ALL TIMES THE MINIMUM
REQUIREMENTS OF THE ABOVE
PARAGRAPHS SHALL BE MET.

If you are familiar with the flaws of Laissez Faire
Capitalism (and I suspect that a lot of people are
not), you can easily understand why high
progressive taxation is required to "tame" LFC. As
things stand now, several bad things happen
continuously and automatically: the nations wealth
steadily and automatically "trickles up" (actually, it
is more like a flood) to the very richest households
(less than 1% of us). Because of their lock on the
wealth, these households automatically have
astronomical investment incomes. The nations
income is thereby concentrated at the top (to folks
who reinvest most of their income instead of
consuming the goods available). The lower 99%

vary from some fairly affluent households near the top to dozens of millions of very poor households at the bottom. In spite of an obvious need, production is curtailed because there is no need to produce stuff for people who can't buy it anyway (no job, no money). Locks in a weak economy, with chronic unemployment and under employment.

What, you might ask, do we do with the internal revenue obtained by "soaking the rich"? BY THE WAY, DON'T FEEL BAD ABOUT "SOAKING THE RICH". THEY DON'T REALLLY "EARN" IT ANYWAY; AS EXPLAINED ABOVE, IT IS AN AUTOMATIC RESULT OF LAISSEZ FAIRE CAPITALISM, AND THE ONLY WAY TO CURE IT IS TO LIMIT THE GROWTH WITH PROGRESSIVE TAXATION. THE ULTRA RICH FAMILY IS ACTUALLY UNABLE TO USE ONE THOUSAND TO THIRTY THOUSAND TIMES AN AVERAGE INCOME ANYWAY! THEY CAN'T AND DON'T EAT THOUSANDS OF TIMES MORE HAMBURGERS THAN THE REST OF US, etc. AFTER A FEW FABULOUS VACATIONS AND A MANSION OR TWO, THEY JUST REINVEST MOST OF IT SO THAT THEY WILL BE EVEN RICHER NEXT YEAR.

So what do you use the revenue for? Why you use it for public "stimulus" programs, of course. That course of action takes some expenses off the poverty stricken folks backs at the same time that the "stimulus" effect provides economic growth and more, better paying, jobs. Appropriate programs are Social Security, Universal Health Care (enhanced medicare for everyone), enhanced and really effective FEMA, enhanced and really effective border patrol, and a host of other things including public transportation and education. Pay off and permanently retire the national debt, and deflate the currency when and as appropriate. You will find that this is now a self regulating system, with long term stability. Takes a load off the States, which then need less revenue. For proof of the above principles, carefully and thoroughly review the economic history of the Roaring 20s, Great Depression, World War II, and the two decades following WWII.

Duard L Pruitt

Revised December 2013

www.ingramcontent.com/pod-product-compliance
Lightning Source LLC
Chambersburg PA
CBHW070459290526
45790CB00003B/1025